Soups, Sandwiches and Wraps

Bonnie Scott

Copyright © 2013 Bonnie Scott

All rights reserved.

ISBN-13: 978-1481997799

TABLE OF CONTENTS

FALL AND WINTER SOUPS

MISC. SOUPS

SOUP CROUTONS

CHILI

Soups, Sandwiches & Wraps

Soup and sandwiches are two anytime foods that you can dress up for company and serve at the dining table with all your best china or eat around a campfire in tin cups and paper plates. Whatever recipes you choose, a sandwich and a bowl of soup is a meal that appeals to anyone, anytime and anywhere.

Soup is not only healthful and delicious, but it makes an easy workday for the cook. Most recipes don't require a lot of prep time or constant monitoring, so they're great for busy days when cooking time is at a premium.

Some soups need to simmer for hours to develop the depth of flavors, while others are ready in less than a half hour. Add or subtract ingredients to make them your own special creations. Soups are so adaptable, and they're perfect for beginners who are just learning how to cook. They're no-fail concoctions that are hard to mess up.

Toppings for your soups let everyone have a choice. Croutons, popcorn, crackers, grated cheese, sour cream, fresh herbs, bacon bits and toasted nuts are just a few of the toppings you can have available for your hungry crew. Other toppings like hot sauce, chives, sliced green onion, lime or lemon slices and crème fraiche add even more texture and flavor to your latest creation.

Sandwiches are great when it's too hot to cook or when mealtime is a staggered affair for folks who can't all make it to the table at the same time. Make-ahead sandwiches and spreads are perfect for our busy lifestyle, so everyone can have a nutritious and flavorful meal or snack when it's most convenient.

Spreads can be used with anything handy. From pita bread to bagels, tortillas, crackers and focaccia, sandwich spreads are perfect to have in the refrigerator for impromptu meals, lunch sacks and appetizers. Properly stored in your refrigerator, sandwich spreads typically last for two or three days.

Deli lunchmeats are also a mainstay for sandwiches. With all the varieties available today, there's never a reason to be caught unprepared when someone asks, "What's for lunch?"

Wraps are just a newfangled way to make a sandwich. This variation uses flat breads, crepes, tortillas, rice paper wrappers and even lettuce leaves to hold the filling. They're great for carb and calorie counters, and it's a great way to use up leftovers and introduce more veggies in your diet.

All sorts of meats, spreads, cheeses and vegetables are used in making wraps. Think outside of the box and use your imagination to create tasty and nutritious wraps. Your family may never even realize they're eating healthy!

When you're armed with these easy-to-make soup, sandwich and wrap recipes, you'll never be at a loss for a quick solution for a tasty meal. A great thing about soups and sandwiches is that they can be used for almost any occasion. Whether it's a quick lunch on the go, a buffet for casual entertaining or a relaxing meal at the end of a busy day, put a soothing soup and tasty wrap on the menu, sit back, and enjoy the compliments.

SPICY SOUPS

"It's better to have no spoon than to have no soup." - German Proverb

Texas Taco Soup

1 lb. hamburger
3 (15 oz. each) cans pinto beans
1 (15 oz.) can Mexican corn
1 (6 oz.) can Ro-Tel tomatoes
2 (15 oz.) cans stewed tomatoes
1 (1 oz.) package dry taco seasoning
1 (1 oz.) package dry ranch dressing
1/2 cup water
Shredded cheddar cheese
Crushed tortilla chips

In a skillet, brown hamburger. In a large soup pot, add hamburger, pinto beans, Mexican corn, tomatoes, stewed tomatoes, dry seasonings and water.

Heat and serve, topped with shredded cheddar cheese and crushed tortilla chips.

Yield: 8 bowls of soup.

PIZZA SOUP

4 (10.75 oz. each) cans tomato soup
2 (15 oz) cans Italian-style diced tomatoes
1 (14 oz.) jar pizza sauce
1 (16 oz.) package spiral noodles, cooked
1 lb. Italian sausage
1 (5 oz.) package mini pepperoni
1 small green pepper, chopped
1 (4 oz.) can sliced mushrooms
1/2 onion, diced
1 (16 oz.) package shredded mozzarella cheese

Prepare noodles as directed on package. In a skillet, brown Italian sausage and drain. In a large saucepan, add tomato soup and Italian tomatoes. Stir in pizza sauce, cooked noodles, pepperoni, sausage, green pepper, onion and mushrooms.

Simmer for 20 minutes. Sprinkle each serving with shredded cheese.

Yield: 12 to 15 servings.

Fiery Tortilla Soup

Garlic (4 fresh cloves chopped or 1/2 teaspoon dry, minced)
1/4 - 1/2 cup onion, chopped
3 - 4 jalapeno peppers, sliced (wear gloves)
Vegetable oil or olive oil
1 (13 oz.) can tomato puree
1 (48 oz.) can chicken broth
1 tablespoon cumin
1 tablespoon oregano
1 tablespoon chili powder
Salt and pepper
Flour tortillas
Grated cheddar cheese

In a large soup kettle, sauté garlic, onion and peppers in oil. Add tomatoes, chicken broth and spices, cook over medium heat for at least 30 minutes.

Slice flour tortillas into strips. Fry in oil until brown and crispy. Do a few at a time and lay on paper towels to drain.

Put prepared tortilla strips in the bottom of soup bowls, pour hot soup over and sprinkle with cheese.

Spicy Sausage Soup

1 lb. regular loose sausage
1 lb. spicy hot loose sausage
3 green bell peppers, diced
1 large onion, diced
1 clove garlic, diced
1/2 cup fresh parsley
Salt and pepper to taste
1 (28 oz.) can diced tomatoes
1 (10.5 oz.) can chicken broth
6 cups water
1 (12 oz.) package bow-tie noodles

In a skillet, fry sausage until brown. Add remaining ingredients. Simmer for 1 hour.

After an hour, add the cooked bow-tie noodles and serve.

POTATO SOUPS

"He who has once burnt his mouth always blows his soup." - German proverb

Creamy Baked Potato Soup

12 slices bacon, cooked and crumbled
2/3 cup flour
2/3 cup butter
7 cups milk
4 potatoes, baked
4 green onions and tops, chopped
1 cup sour cream
1 1/4 cups cheddar cheese, shredded
1 teaspoon black pepper
1 teaspoon salt

Peel baked potatoes and cut into cubes; set aside. In a large pot, melt the butter over medium heat. Add flour, whisking until smooth. Slowly stir in milk; use a whisk to mix until thickened. Add the onions and potato cubes. Bring to a boil and stir frequently.

Reduce the heat and cook for 15 minutes more. Mix in sour cream, cheese, bacon, salt and pepper. Continue cooking, stirring frequently, until cheese is melted.

Potato Cheese Soup

4 cups chopped potatoes
4 cups water
1 cup carrots, cut small
2 teaspoons onion, minced
4 chicken bouillon cubes
1/4 teaspoon pepper (optional)
8 oz. cheddar cheese

In a soup kettle, cover potatoes, carrots, onion, bouillon cubes and pepper with water. Bring to a boil; cover and cook until vegetables are soft.

Once soft, mash the veggies and potatoes in the soup with a potato masher. Stir in cheese. Cook until cheese is melted.

IRISH POTATO SOUP

4 teaspoons margarine
2 onions
5 1/2 cups chicken broth
3 cups milk
2 lbs. potatoes
1 1/4 teaspoon dried thyme
1/2 teaspoon celery seeds
1/4 cup fresh chives, chopped
1 cup light cream
Salt and pepper

Roux:
2 teaspoons margarine
2 teaspoons all-purpose flour

Garnishes:
1/2 cup fresh chives, chopped
6 slices microwave bacon, crisp and broken into pieces

Peel and slice the potatoes. Heat a large soup kettle and add the margarine and onion and cook until onions are tender. Add the chicken stock, milk and potatoes. Mix in the thyme, celery seeds and chives. Cook, covered, on medium-low heat for one hour.

Make the roux: Melt the margarine in a small saucepan and stir in the flour. Let the mixture boil for 2 minutes on medium-low heat, stirring constantly. Whisk the roux into the soup to thicken. Cook for 10 minutes. Add the cream and reheat, but do not boil. Season with salt and pepper. Serve with the garnishes above.

Easy Potato Soup

3 cups frozen hash browns
1 small onion
1 1/4 cups chicken broth
1 tablespoon cornstarch
2 cups milk
3/4 teaspoon salt
1/3 (15 oz.) jar processed cheese sauce or 1 cup shredded cheese
1 tablespoon dried parsley
2 tablespoons margarine
1 (15 oz.) can mixed vegetables
1 cup cubed ham

In a 2-quart saucepan, mix potatoes, onion, and broth. Heat to boiling; cover. Turn heat to low and cook gently 3 to 5 minutes until potatoes are tender. Mix cornstarch with a little milk, blending until smooth. Combine with remaining milk; add salt. Stir into potato mixture. Heat to boiling, stirring until mixture is smooth and slightly thickened.

Remove from heat; add cheese, parsley, and margarine. Stir until cheese and margarine are melted. Add heated ham and vegetables. Cook until hot.

Yield: 4 to 5 servings.

Sweet Potato Soup

3 large sweet potatoes
1 cup chicken broth
1/2 cup water
1/4 cup orange juice
1/4 teaspoon ground nutmeg
1/4 teaspoon salt
1 cup milk

Peel and chop the sweet potatoes. Put the sweet potatoes in a 2-quart saucepan, and cover with chicken broth and water. Cover and heat to boiling; reduce heat. Simmer 30 to 35 minutes or until the sweet potatoes are tender.

Place potatoes in blender or food processor. Add 1/2 cup of the broth. Cover and blend until smooth. Put blended mixture back in pan. Stir in the rest of broth, juice, nutmeg and salt. Cook over medium heat, stirring frequently until hot. Stir in the milk and continue cooking until hot.

Yield: 4 servings.

Original Potato Soup

10 medium potatoes
2 medium carrots
1/2 medium onion
Milk
1/2 lb. bacon
Salt
Pepper

Pare and slice potatoes. In a large saucepan, add potatoes and enough salted water to cover potatoes and a little bit over. Bring to a boil.

Cook and crumble bacon; add to potato mixture. Slice and quarter carrots and onion; add to mixture. Simmer on medium heat until potatoes and veggies are tender. Add milk to desired consistency and simmer for 1 hour. Salt and pepper to taste.

Microwave Potato Soup

3 to 4 slices bacon
6 medium potatoes, cubed
1 medium onion, chopped
2 cups water
1/4 teaspoon curry powder
1 1/2 teaspoon salt
1/8 teaspoon pepper
5 teaspoons flour
2 cups milk
1/3 cup cheddar cheese, shredded

Place bacon slices in a 4-quart casserole dish. Microwave until bacon is crisp. Remove bacon and set dish and bacon grease aside. Add potatoes, onion, water, curry powder, salt and pepper to bacon drippings. Cover and microwave 12-15 minutes.

Combine flour and milk and mix until smooth. Stir into vegetables. Microwave uncovered for 12 to 14 minutes until mixture thickens, stirring a few times. Stir in shredded cheddar cheese until melted. Crumble bacon and use as garnish on soup.

German Potato Soup

4 slices diced bacon
4 large onions, chopped
2 tablespoons flour
4 chicken bouillon cubes
4 cups hot water
Salt and freshly ground pepper to taste
4 peeled sliced large new potatoes
2 egg yolks
1 cup sour cream
1 tablespoon chopped fresh parsley

In a deep saucepan, sauté diced bacon until it is curly. Add chopped onions and sauté in flour; mix well and cook a minute or two. Crumble in bouillon cubes and add hot water, stirring constantly. Add salt and pepper and sliced potatoes.

Simmer for 8 minutes or until the potato slices are barely tender. Whisk egg yolks with sour cream and whisk in a little hot soup to this mixture. Add this sour cream mixture to the saucepan of soup and continue to heat. Add parsley, stir, bring just to the boiling point and serve piping hot.

Potato Sausage Soup

1 lb. Italian sausage
1/2 cup onion, chopped
2 (16 oz. each) cans tomatoes
4 (6 cups) potatoes, pared and diced
2 beef bouillon cubes
1/4 cup parsley, chopped
1 cup celery, sliced
2 tablespoons celery leaves, chopped
1 1/2 cups water
1 bay leaf
1 teaspoon salt
1/2 teaspoon thyme
1/4 teaspoon pepper
1 tablespoon lemon juice

In a large saucepan or kettle, brown sliced sausage over medium heat. Add chopped onion and cook 5 minutes. Add tomatoes, potatoes, bouillon cubes, parsley, celery, celery leaves, water, bay leaf, salt, thyme, pepper and lemon juice. Bring to a boil and cook until potatoes are tender.

Yield: 6 servings.

Cream of Potato Soup

2 tablespoons margarine
2 teaspoons flour
2 cups milk
1 cup cooked potatoes, peeled and diced
1/4 teaspoon salt
Pepper to taste
1 stalk cooked celery, chopped
1 cooked carrot, chopped

Melt the margarine in a medium saucepan on medium-low heat. Add the flour and whisk until smooth. Cook the butter mixture for one minute, stirring constantly. Slowly add the milk.

Cook on medium-high heat, stirring constantly until thickened. Stir in potatoes, salt and pepper, celery and carrot. Cook 5 minutes or until hot.

Yield: 2 1/2 cups.

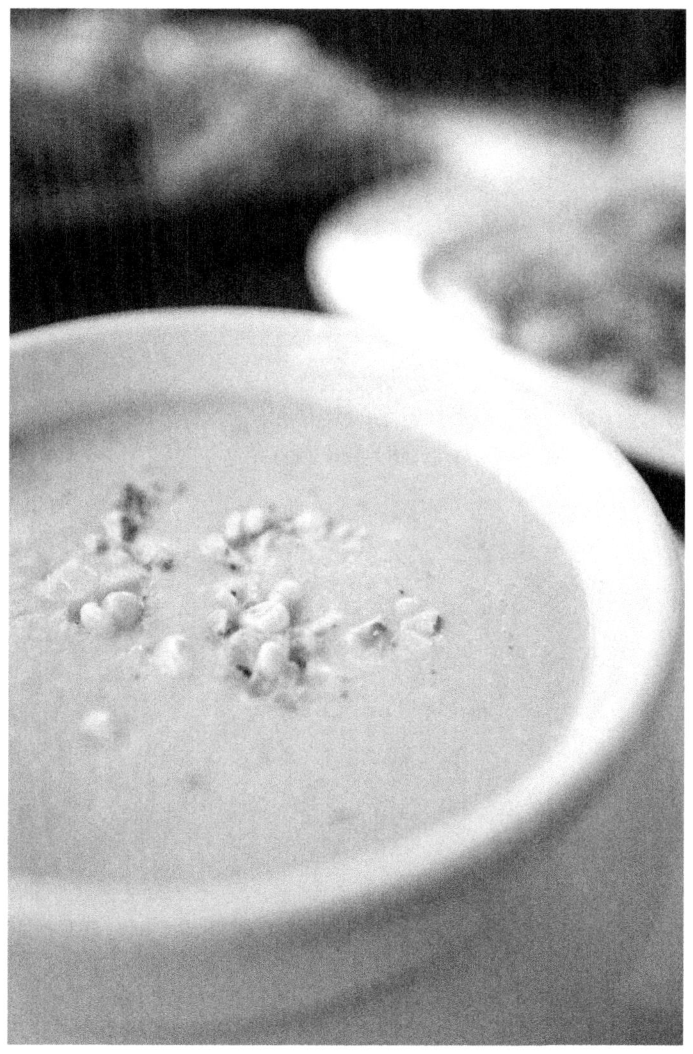

CHOWDERS

Which hand should you use to stir the soup?

Neither, you should use a spoon.

Quick Corn Chowder

6 - 8 slices bacon, diced and fried
2 teaspoons bacon fat

Add:

1 (10.5 oz.) can cream of potato soup
1 (10.5 oz.) can French onion soup
1 (15.25 oz.) can whole kernel corn
2 cups milk

Heat and serve.

Quick Tuna Cheese Chowder

2 medium carrots, grated
1 medium onion, chopped
1/4 cup margarine
1/4 cup flour
2 cups milk (can use skim)
2 cups chicken broth
1 (5 oz.) can tuna, drained and flaked
1/2 teaspoon Worcestershire sauce
1/2 teaspoon celery seed
1 cup shredded American cheese

In a 3-quart saucepan, cook carrots and onion in margarine until onion is tender, but not brown. Mix in flour; add milk and chicken broth. Cook and stir until thickened.

Stir in tuna, Worcestershire sauce and celery seed; heat through. Add cheese. Heat and stir until the cheese is melted.

New England Clam Chowder

1/4 lb. salt pork, cubed
1 onion, chopped
2 celery stalks, chopped
2 cups hot water
3 large potatoes, diced
1 carrot, cut in small pieces
1 (8 oz.) jar clam juice
3 (6.5 oz. each) cans chopped or minced clams
Salt and pepper to taste

In a large soup kettle, sauté onion, celery and pork; remove pork. Add water, potatoes, and carrot; cook until tender. Add clam juice, clams, salt, and pepper.

White sauce:

2 cups milk
1 teaspoon salt
White pepper

Blend the white sauce and add to the preceding ingredients. Keep warm, but do not boil. Garnish with a sprig of parsley.

Easy Sausage Chowder

1 lb. beef sausage, cut in small pieces
1 medium onion, finely chopped
4 cups potatoes, diced
3 cups water
2 teaspoons dried parsley
1 teaspoon basil
1 teaspoon salt
1/8 teaspoon pepper
1 (15.25 oz.) can whole kernel corn
1 (14.75 oz.) can cream-style corn
1 (12 oz.) can evaporated skim milk

Cook sausage and onion in a large skillet until onion is transparent. Add potatoes, water, parsley, basil, salt and pepper. Cook until potatoes are tender.

Add corn and milk. Heat until hot.

Corn Chowder with Ham

2 cups water
2 cups potatoes, peeled and diced
1/2 cup celery, chopped
1/2 cup carrots, chopped
1/4 cup onions, chopped
1 cup ham, diced
2 teaspoons salt
1/2 teaspoon pepper
1 (14.75 oz.) can cream-style corn
1 cup Velveeta cheese, cubed

White Sauce:

1/4 cup butter
1/4 cup flour
2 cups milk

In a large soup kettle, simmer potatoes, celery, carrots, onions, ham, salt and pepper in water until tender. While that is cooking, make white sauce: melt butter; add flour then cook for one minute; add milk and whisk or stir with a slotted spoon as to not get lumpy.

Continue cooking, stirring constantly until smooth and thickened. Add white sauce to vegetables. Do not boil. Add cream style corn and cubed Velveeta cheese. Heat until cheese is melted.

Two Bean Chowder

1 cup dry great northern beans
1 cup dry red beans
2 quarts water
1 smoked ham hock
1 cup onion, chopped
1 clove garlic minced
3/4 cup diced or grated celery
3/4 cup diced or grated carrots
Dash red pepper
1 1/2 cups milk
Salt and pepper to taste

Wash and soak beans overnight or bring to boil and let stand 1 hour. Drain beans. In a soup kettle with 2 quarts of water, add beans and ham hock, cover, let simmer 1 1/2 hours.

Remove ham hock, cut in small pieces. Mash a cup of the beans. Return meat and mashed beans to soup, add onion, garlic, celery, carrots, red pepper, and simmer 1 hour. Add milk and heat. Season to taste.

Yield: 6 to 8 servings.

Basic Clam Chowder

2 large potatoes, cubed
1 stalk celery, chopped
1/4 cup onion, chopped
1 1/2 teaspoons salt
1/8 teaspoon pepper
1/8 teaspoon thyme
2 teaspoons butter or margarine
1/4 cup flour
3 cups milk
4 (6 oz. each) cans minced clams (reserve liquid)
6 slices bacon, fried and crumbled

In a large saucepan, combine potatoes, celery, onions, salt, pepper, thyme and clam liquid. Bring to a boil and cook for about 10 minutes, until the veggies are tender. Slowly stir milk into flour and add to vegetables.

Cook over medium heat until thickened. Stir in clams, bacon and butter. Continue cooking until heated through. Do not boil.

Bacon Corn Chowder

5 bacon slices
1 medium onion thinly sliced
2 large potatoes, peeled and diced
1/2 cup water
2 cups milk
1 (14.75 oz.) can cream-style corn
1 teaspoon salt
1/8 teaspoon pepper

In a large pan, cook bacon until crisp. Remove bacon and set aside. Leave 4 tablespoons bacon grease in the pan. Add onion slices to pan and cook until light brown. Add diced potato and water; cook over medium heat until potato is tender, 10 to 15 minutes.

Mix in milk, cream corn, salt and pepper; cook until heated through. Add crumbled bacon to each soup serving.

CHICKEN SOUPS

"Old chickens make the best soup." - French proverb

Chicken Noodle Vegetable Soup

1 (48 oz.) can chicken broth
1 onion, finely chopped
2 celery stalks, thinly sliced
2 carrots, thinly sliced
2 zucchini, thinly sliced
1 tablespoon parsley
2 oz. very thin egg noodles
1/2 cup cooked chicken, shredded or cubed
Salt and pepper

In a large saucepan on medium heat, simmer the chicken broth just until it starts to boil. Add the onion, celery and carrots and continue to simmer about 10 minutes until the vegetables are slightly soft. Add the parsley and zucchini and cook 15 more minutes.

Add the chicken to the soup. Add the noodles and cook until the noodles are just tender, 3 to 4 minutes, or according to the package directions. Add salt and pepper to taste.

Yield: 4 servings.

Chicken Tomato Soup

2 teaspoons butter or oil
1 large onion, chopped
4 oz. cream cheese
30 oz. tomato sauce
4 cups milk
2 cloves garlic, chopped
3 cubes chicken bouillon
1 deboned chicken, cooked and cut into pieces
3 tomatoes, chopped
1 teaspoon hot sauce
1 teaspoon anise
2 zucchini, chopped

In a large saucepan on medium heat, melt butter or oil and sauté chopped onion. Stir in cream cheese. Add tomato sauce, milk, garlic, chicken bouillon, chicken, tomatoes, hot sauce and anise.

Add zucchini 30 minutes before serving the soup.

Chicken Tortellini Soup

3 (10.5 oz., each) cans condensed chicken broth
6 cups water
1 (10.5 oz.) can cream of chicken soup
2 cups cooked chicken, cubed
1 cup carrots, sliced
1 cup onion, chopped
2 garlic cloves, minced
1/2 teaspoon basil
1/2 teaspoon oregano
1 (7 oz.) package cheese tortellini
1 (9 oz.) package frozen cut broccoli, thawed
Grated parmesan cheese

In a large saucepan, combine chicken broth, water, soup, chicken, carrots, onions, garlic, basil and oregano; bring to a boil. Add tortellini and simmer uncovered for 30 minutes.

Add broccoli and simmer for an additional 5 to 10 minutes or until broccoli is just tender.

Serve with Parmesan cheese.

Chicken Noodle Soup

2 1/2 to 3 lb. chicken
2 stalks celery, diced
2 carrots, diced
1 onion, chopped
Bay leaf
1 tablespoon dried parsley
2 chicken bouillon cubes
8 cups water
1 (12 oz.) package egg noodles
Salt
Pepper

In a large saucepan, cook chicken with celery, carrots, onion, bay leaf, parsley and bouillon cubes in 2 quarts of water. Bring to a boil, reduce heat and simmer for 40 minutes. Remove chicken from broth to cool.

Remove meat from the bone and skim fat from broth. (The easiest way to skim the broth is to cook the chicken a day before and let broth cool overnight. The fat will be on the top of the broth and easy to remove.) Return chicken to skimmed broth and add noodles. Add salt and pepper. Cook until noodles are done.

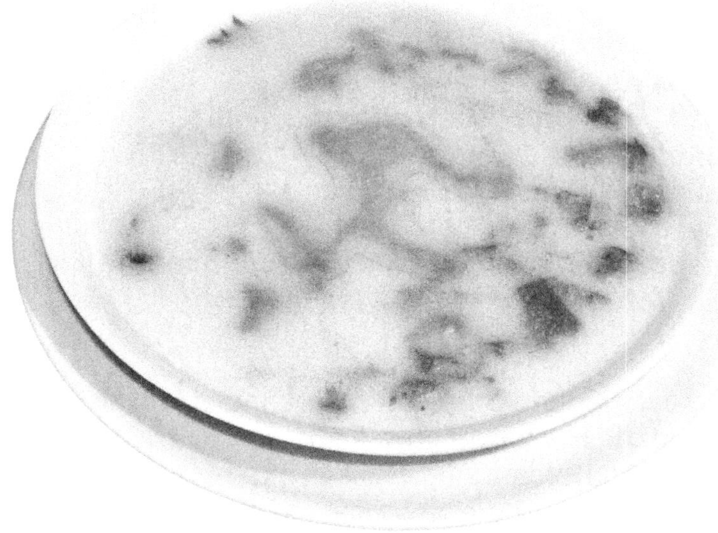

CHEESY SOUPS

What do ducks have for lunch?

Soup and quackers.

Cheese and Beer Soup

1/2 cup margarine
1 cup flour
4 cups chicken broth
1 1/2 cups heavy cream
1 (16 oz.) jar of processed cheese sauce
1/2 cup chives
1 teaspoon Worcestershire sauce
6 oz. beer
1/2 teaspoon yellow food coloring (optional)
Popcorn for topping

In a large saucepan, melt the margarine and whisk in flour until blended. Heat over low flame for 5 minutes, stirring frequently. Add cream and chicken broth; mix until soup is thick and smooth. Add cheese sauce and stir until cheese is melted and soup is smooth. Add chives, Worcestershire sauce, beer, food coloring and chives.

Simmer for 15 minutes, stirring constantly. Top with popcorn.

Yield: 8 servings.

Broccoli Cheese Soup

3/4 cup onions, chopped
2 tablespoons margarine
7 chicken bouillon cubes
6 cups water
8 oz. fine egg noodles,
2 (12 oz.) packages frozen broccoli florets, chopped
1 teaspoon salt
1/8 teaspoon garlic powder
1/8 teaspoon pepper
6 cups milk
1 lb. American cheese, cubed or grated

In a large saucepan, sauté onions in margarine for 3 minutes. Add bouillon cubes and water. Heat to boiling, stirring until bouillon cubes are dissolved. Add noodles, broccoli, garlic powder and salt.

Cook for 7 minutes or until noodles are done. Add pepper, milk and cheese; continue cooking until cheese melts, stirring occasionally.

Yield: 10 servings.

Cheese Soup

2 tablespoons onion, chopped
4 tablespoons butter or margarine
4 tablespoons flour
1/4 teaspoon dry mustard
2 cups milk
2 cups bouillon or chicken broth
2 cups grated cheddar cheese

In a large saucepan, brown onion in butter; blend in flour and dry mustard. Gradually stir in milk and broth. Bring to a boil and boil for 1 minute, stirring constantly. Add cheese and stir until melted.

Canadian Cheese Soup

1/2 cup margarine
1/2 cup onion, minced
1 cup carrots, finely diced
1 1/2 cups celery, finely chopped
2 cups chicken broth
1/2 cup flour
6 cups milk
4 cups cheddar cheese, grated
Minced parsley

Melt margarine in a large saucepan. Add onion, cook until tender. Add carrots, celery and broth. Cover and simmer for 15 minutes.

Make a paste with flour and 1 cup of milk. Add to vegetable mixture. Add remaining milk, cook, stirring constantly until slightly thickened. Add cheese and stir over low heat until melted. Garnish with parsley and serve hot.

Yield: 10 to 12 servings.

Bubba's Beer Cheese Soup

2 quarts milk
2 teaspoon salt
1/4 teaspoon pepper white
1/4 teaspoon garlic salt
Roux (recipe follows)
1 (16 oz.) jar processed cheese sauce
8 oz. beer

Roux is made by mixing 1 cup butter and 1 1/2 cups flour.

In a large saucepan, warm milk just to a simmer; don't boil. Add salt, pepper and garlic. Add roux until soup is desired thickness. Whip smooth, using wire whip.

Meanwhile, put jar of cheese sauce in a saucepan of hot water. Stir until cheese is thin enough to pour. Add cheese sauce and whip thoroughly. Stir in beer. Keep warm over low heat.

Yield: 8 to 12 servings.

Cheddar Cheese Soup

1/2 cup diced bacon
1 cup celery, finely chopped
1 cup onion, chopped
1 cup carrot, finely chopped
3/4 cup green pepper, finely chopped
3 cups canned diluted chicken broth
1 1/2 cups beer
3 1/2 cups milk
2/3 cup flour
4 cups cheddar cheese, shredded
1/2 cup whipping cream
1/2 teaspoon salt
1/4 teaspoon white pepper

Cook bacon in a Dutch oven until crisp; remove bacon, leaving the bacon drippings in the Dutch oven. Set the bacon aside.

Sauté celery, onion, carrots, and green pepper in bacon drippings until onion is tender. Stir in chicken broth and beer. Bring to a boil; reduce heat and simmer until vegetables are tender. Remove from heat and set aside. Combine milk and flour in a saucepan, stirring well. Cook over medium heat until thickened, stirring constantly.

Add cheese mixture to broth mixture. Mix in whipping cream, salt, and pepper. Top individual serving bowls with reserved bacon pieces.

Yield: 10 cups.

Cheesy Vegetable Soup

2 (16 oz., each) packages frozen cauliflower, broccoli and carrot mix
1 (32 oz.) box fat free chicken broth
1 (10 oz.) can Ro-Tel diced tomatoes and green chiles mild
1 (10 oz.) package Velveeta cheese

In a large saucepan, add frozen vegetables, chicken broth and tomatoes. Bring to a boil. Simmer for 4 to 5 minutes until vegetables are tender. Remove from heat.

Cut cheese into chunks and add to the soup. Stir until the cheese is melted and heated through.

VEGGIE SOUPS

"I once cut my mouth on my wife's soup."

Milton Berle

Vegetable Soup

1 package soup bones (short ribs)
1 lb. stew meat, cut in bite size pieces
1/2 large onion, chopped
2 stalks celery, chopped
1 lb. bag carrots, sliced
1 (12 oz.) package frozen vegetables or just frozen corn
4 medium potatoes, peeled and cubed
Salt and pepper
Paprika
1 tablespoon parsley flakes
3 beef bouillon cubes

Rinse off soup bone. Put stew meat and soup bone in a large pot and cover with water until about 2" from the top of pot. Turn to medium heat until it starts to boil. Remove scum from water. Turn heat to simmer. Add salt and pepper. Sprinkle top of water with paprika. Add the onion and celery. Mix in parsley flakes, bouillon cubes and carrots.

Add package of frozen vegetables and potatoes the last 2 hours before soup is done. More salt may be needed. Cook all day long on simmer.

Pumpkin Vegetable Soup

1 large onion, chopped
2 teaspoons margarine
4 cups chicken broth, reduced-sodium
2 medium potatoes, peeled and cubed
2 carrots, chopped
1 cup cooked lima beans, fresh or frozen
1 cup corn, fresh or frozen
2 celery ribs, chopped
1/4 teaspoon white pepper
1/2 teaspoon salt
1/4 teaspoon ground nutmeg
1 (15 oz.) can solid pack pumpkin

Sauté onion in margarine until tender in a large saucepan. Add the broth, potatoes, carrots, corn, lima beans and celery; bring it to a boil. Reduce the heat, cover, simmer for 30 minutes or until veggies are tender.

Stir in pumpkin, salt, pepper and nutmeg. Cook 5 to 10 minutes longer or until heated through. For a smooth soup, run through a puree stage in blender and reheat to serve.

Yield: 7 servings.

Vegetable Beef Barley Soup

2 1/2 lbs. beef shank
3 teaspoons salt
1/2 teaspoon pepper
3 beef bouillon cubes
1 bay leaf
2 quarts water
3/4 cup barley
2 large potatoes, diced
2 large carrots, diced
2 stalks celery diced
1/2 cup onion, chopped
1 (16 oz.) can tomatoes, chopped

In a large saucepan, boil beef, salt, pepper, bouillon, bay leaf and water for approximately 2 hours. Remove beef from bone; add to stock, then add remaining ingredients. Boil for 1 more hour.

Low Calorie Vegetable Soup

8 cups water
1 (46 oz.) can tomato juice
10 beef bouillon cubes
4 stalks celery, chopped
1/2 head cabbage, shredded
6 large carrots
1 1/2 teaspoons onion flakes

Mix all ingredients in a large saucepan, and simmer 2 to 3 hours.

Homemade Vegetable Beef Soup

1 lb. chopped beef
2 cups fresh string beans
2 cups fresh butter beans
2 cups garden peas
2 cups field peas
1/4 cup rice
1 cup chopped carrots
2 cups chopped okra
2 cups corn
1 cup chopped bell pepper
1 cup chopped mushrooms
1/4 cup cooking oil
1/2 cup sugar
2 cups chopped tomatoes

In a large saucepan, cook beef about 30 minutes. Add the remaining ingredients and simmer for about one hour.

TOMATO SOUPS

"Troubles are easier to take with soup than without."

Yiddish saying

Creamy Tomato Basil Soup

3/4 cup butter
2 teaspoons olive oil
1 large onion
4 basil leaves, chopped (or 1/2 teaspoon dried basil)
2 sprigs fresh thyme (or 1/2 teaspoon dried thyme)
1/2 teaspoon salt
Pepper to taste
2 1/2 lbs. fresh ripe tomatoes, cored (or 1 2-lb. 3 oz. can of Italian style tomatoes)
1 (6 oz.) can tomato paste
1/4 cup flour
1 3/4 cups low-fat milk
1 (14.5 oz.) can chicken broth
1 1/2 teaspoons sugar
1 1/4 cups half and half
Croutons, optional

Heat 1/2 cup of the butter in a soup pot; add olive oil. Add onion, basil, thyme, salt and pepper. Stir occasionally until onion is wilted. Mix in the tomatoes and tomato paste. Simmer for 10 minutes.

In a separate bowl, mix flour and 5 tablespoons of milk. Add to the tomato mixture. Add remaining milk, chicken broth, sugar and half and half, and simmer 30 minutes. Top with croutons if desired.

Yield: 8 servings.

Creamy Tomato Basil Soup

Tomato Soup

1 (10.5 oz.) can chicken broth
1 (32 oz.) can diced tomatoes
2 teaspoons sugar
1 teaspoon butter
1 onion, chopped
1/8 teaspoon baking soda
2 cups cream or half and half

In a large saucepan, combine broth, tomatoes, sugar, butter, onions and baking soda. Simmer for 1 hour. Heat cream in a double boiler. Add tomato mixture to cream.

Jamaican Tomato Soup

2 (15 oz.) cans stewed tomatoes
1 (15 oz.) can tomato puree or sauce
1 cup orange juice
Dried or fresh basil to taste
Dried or fresh cilantro to taste
Dried or fresh parsley to taste
1 (15 oz.) can mandarin oranges, drained

In a large saucepan, heat together stewed tomatoes and tomato puree or sauce, orange juice and herbs. Simmer until flavors blend, about 30 minutes.

Add mandarin oranges and heat until the oranges begin to break up. Serve with a dollop of sour cream.

MEAT SOUPS

What's the difference between roast beef and pea soup?

Anyone can roast beef.

Mini-Meatball Soup

1 lb. lean ground beef
1 egg
1/2 cup Italian breadcrumbs
1/3 cup grated parmesan cheese
1 teaspoon garlic powder
1/2 medium Spanish onion chopped + 1/4 onion minced
Black pepper to taste
Salt to taste
1 carrot, chopped
1 stalk celery, chopped
2 cloves garlic, minced
2 teaspoons extra virgin olive oil
1/4 teaspoon ground nutmeg
45 oz. no-fat low sodium chicken broth
1/2 cup small pasta
Handful fresh parsley chopped

Preheat oven to 375 degrees F. Combine meat, egg, breadcrumbs, cheese, garlic powder, minced onion, salt, and pepper. Form 1/2-inch mini meatballs and place on a nonstick baking sheet. Bake for 12 minutes at 375 degrees F. to brown balls.

While meatballs are cooking, sauté chopped carrot, celery, onion, and garlic in olive oil over medium heat in a soup pot or deep-frying pan. Sprinkle vegetables with nutmeg, salt, and pepper. Cook 5 minutes. Add broth and turn heat up to high. When broth boils, drop in pasta. Reduce heat to simmer.

Cook 8 to 10 minutes, until pasta is cooked. Drop in meatballs and parsley and serve with bread and a salad.

January Ham Soup

2 tablespoons butter
2 cups carrots, cut in 1-inch chunks
2 cups celery, cut in 1-inch chunks
1 cup onions, sliced
32 oz. chicken broth
1 tablespoon Worcestershire sauce
1 cup dried lentils
1 1/2 cups milk
1 1/2 cups ham, finely chopped
1 1/2 tablespoons flour
1/2 teaspoon powdered mustard
1 egg, slightly beaten

In a large, heavy saucepot or Dutch oven, melt butter. Add carrots, celery and onions. Sauté for 5 minutes. Add chicken broth, Worcestershire sauce and lentils. Bring to a boil. Reduce heat and simmer, covered, until lentils are cooked, about 1 1/2 hours. Stir in milk. Cook and stir until hot.

Mix ham with flour, mustard and egg. Shape into 1-inch balls. Drop in hot soup. Cover and simmer until dumplings are cooked, about 15 minutes.

Yield: 2 1/2 quarts.

Hearty Beef Soup

1 lb. ground beef
1 cup onion, chopped
2 cloves garlic, minced
2 teaspoons salt
1/2 teaspoon oregano
1/2 teaspoon pepper
1/4 teaspoon sage
1 lb. tomatoes, cut up
1 cup celery, chopped
1 cup pared potatoes, sliced
1 cup carrots, sliced
1 cup cabbage, chopped
1 cup zucchini, diced
1 (10.5 oz.) can condensed beef broth
2 beef bouillon cubes
4 cups water
1/2 cup barley or uncooked rice

In a large saucepan, brown beef; add onion and garlic. Cook until onions are tender; drain fat. Stir in salt, oregano, pepper, sage, tomatoes and vegetables, broth, bouillon cubes and water.

Bring to a boil; reduce heat. Cover and simmer 30 minutes. Add rice or barley, simmer until tender.

Yield: 2 1/2 quarts.

Easy Meatball Soup

1 lb. ground beef
1 egg
1/2 cup cracker crumbs
2 tablespoons milk
1 teaspoon onion, chopped
Salt and pepper
1/4 cup vegetable oil

Mix the above ingredients together. Make small balls and fry in 1/4 cup oil.

1 (28 oz.) can diced tomatoes
1 (10.75 oz.) can tomato soup
1 can water from tomato soup can
1 (2 oz.) package onion soup mix
1 (12 oz.) frozen package mixed vegetables

In a large saucepan, combine tomatoes, tomato soup, water, onion soup mix and mixed vegetables. Add meatballs and simmer for 15 to 20 minutes.

Yield: 6 servings.

FALL AND WINTER SOUPS

"Only the pure of heart can make good soup."

Beethoven

Pumpkin Bisque

4 teaspoons unsalted butter
1 large onion, chopped
1 large leek, cleaned and chopped
1 lb. pumpkin puree, canned or fresh
1/4 teaspoon ginger
1/4 teaspoon nutmeg
1/4 teaspoon white pepper
4 cups chicken broth
1 cup light cream
8 teaspoons light cream

Melt butter in a large saucepan over medium-high heat. Add leek and onion; sauté until soft, between 5 and 10 minutes.

Mix in the pumpkin, ginger, nutmeg and pepper. Stir in the broth; cook until boiling. Reduce heat and cook for 15 minutes, stirring occasionally. Puree to fine mixture, either in a food processor with the metal blade, or in a blender. Return mixture to saucepan and add 1 cup cream.

Over medium heat, stirring frequently, cook until heated through. When ready to serve, swirl 1 teaspoon of cream into each serving.

Yield: 8 servings.

Butternut Squash Soup

1 medium squash
4 (10.5 oz.) cans chicken broth
3 leeks
1/2 cup butter
1 teaspoon salt
1 teaspoon pepper white
1 teaspoon nutmeg

Garnish:
Plain yogurt
Chopped fresh chive
Crumbled bacon

Wash and split squash; remove seeds and put squash in a glass baking dish. Cover with plastic wrap and microwave on high until squash can be spooned from skin. Remove from skin.

In a large soup kettle over medium-high heat, melt butter. Add salt, pepper, and nutmeg to butter. Add sliced leek, sauté until translucent. Pour chicken broth into pot and simmer for 25 minutes; spoon in squash and simmer another 20 minutes. Remove from stove; let cool and blend. Return to pot, reheat, spoon into individual bowls, garnish with yogurt, chive and bacon and serve.

Mushroom Rice Soup

1/2 cup wild rice, uncooked
1 1/2 cups water
1 medium onion, thinly sliced
1/4 lb. fresh mushrooms, sliced
3 teaspoons butter
1/4 cup flour
4 cups chicken broth
1 cup light cream or half and half
1/4 cup dry sherry
Chopped parsley

Note: Washing wild rice before cooking is recommended. Pour the rice into a colander or sieve and wash it thoroughly under running cold water. Also, wild rice takes more than twice as long as white rice to cook.

Add the rice to 1 1/2 cups water in a saucepan, heat to boiling, lower heat and cover; simmer for one hour.

Cut onion slices into quarters. In a soup pot, sauté onions and mushrooms in butter, until onion is transparent. Add flour and stir, cook for 5 minutes. Stir in chicken stock and bring to a boil, stirring until smooth and flour is cooked. Add the wild rice mixture, cream and sherry, stirring until heated through. Garnish with parsley.

French Onion Soup

6 cups beef broth/bouillon
6 medium onions, sliced
3 teaspoons butter
2 teaspoons flour
Salt and pepper to taste
Fresh French bread, 1" slices
Grated aged Swiss or gruyere cheese

Melt butter in a large skillet. Stir in enough flour to thicken butter and heat until bubbly. Add sliced onions and sauté until soft. Do not brown onions. Add beef broth/bouillon and heat to boiling. Add sautéed onions to broth.

Simmer about 30 minutes. Season to taste. In shallow soup bowls, place one slice bread and ladle enough soup to cover bread. Generously top soup and bread with grated cheese.

Yield: 4 to 6 servings.

Cream of Broccoli Soup

1 medium bunch of broccoli, cut up (4 cups)
1/4 cup onion, chopped
4 teaspoons butter
1/4 cup flour
2 cups chicken broth
2 cups milk
1 teaspoon Worcestershire sauce
1 cup cheddar cheese

Cook broccoli until soft. In a large saucepan, sauté onion in butter. Blend in flour. Add chicken broth, milk and Worcestershire sauce. Cook until thickened. Add cheese and cooked broccoli. Stir to melt cheese.

Quick Corn Soup

1 (14.75) can cream-style corn
2 teaspoons dry parsley
1 green onion
Salt and pepper to taste
1/4 teaspoon garlic powder
1 pint half and half

Put all ingredients in a blender. Set on blend just long enough to mix well. Heat and serve.

Yield: 4 to 6 servings.

CABBAGE SOUP

4 teaspoons butter
4 teaspoons brown sugar
1 head cabbage shredded or 1 16 oz. package of pre-shredded cabbage
4 cups beef or chicken stock
1 teaspoon salt
1/2 teaspoon crushed red pepper
1/2 teaspoon all spice

Combine butter and brown sugar in a large soup pot. Add cabbage and continue to sauté. Combine stock, salt, red pepper, allspice and add to cabbage mixture. Cook until cabbage is soft and soup is hot.

Cream of Carrot Soup

1 lb. carrots, sliced
1 cup onions, chopped
Salt and pepper to taste
2 (14.5 oz., each) cans chicken or beef broth
16 oz. carton of half and half

Simmer carrots and onions in enough broth to cover until tender. Pour into a blender and puree until smooth. Add salt and pepper.

Pour carrot mixture into a saucepan and add enough half and half to make a desired consistency. Reheat slowly on low. To make this recipe low in fat, omit the half & half and use part low fat canned milk and part skim milk.

Zucchini Soup

1 1/2 lbs. sausage (regular or hot)
2 lbs. unpeeled zucchini, sliced into 1/4-inch pieces
2 cups green pepper, cut into 1/2-inch pieces
2 cups celery, cut into 1/2-inch pieces
2 (28 oz., each) cans whole tomatoes
1 1/2 cups onion, chopped
1/2 teaspoon oregano
2 tablespoons sugar
2 teaspoons salt
1 teaspoon garlic powder

Brown sausage in pot; drain grease. Add celery and onions. Cook for 15 minutes, stirring occasionally. Add remaining ingredients and simmer for 1 1/2 hours.

Serve with garlic bread and sprinkle servings with Parmesan cheese.

Creamed Wild Rice Soup

1/4 cup wild rice
4 cups chicken broth
1/2 cup diced celery
1/4 cup diced onion
2 teaspoons thinly sliced mushrooms
1/2 cup diced green pepper
1/4 cup butter
1/2 cup flour
1/2 teaspoon salt
1/4 teaspoon pepper
1/4 teaspoon garlic powder
2 teaspoons silvered almonds
1 teaspoon diced pimiento
2 cups half and half

In a large saucepan or soup pot, cook rice in chicken broth until tender. In a separate pan, sauté celery, onions, mushrooms and green pepper in butter. Add flour and cook for 1 to 2 minutes over low heat; add to cooked rice and broth. Add salt, pepper, garlic powder, almonds and pimiento.

Stir until there are no lumps. Add half and half. Heat and serve. Can add cooked chicken or diced ham, if desired.

Minestrone Soup

1 cup ditalini noodles
1 clove garlic, minced
2 large onions, chopped
4 tablespoons parsley
4 stalks celery, diced
1 tablespoon oil
1 (16 oz.) can tomato sauce
1 (28 oz.) can crushed tomatoes
1 cup cabbage, diced
3 beef cubes
8 cups water
2 teaspoons salt
1/4 teaspoon pepper
1/4 teaspoon celery salt
1/4 teaspoon basil
1 tablespoon soy sauce
1 (15.5 oz.) can kidney beans
1 (15.5 oz.) can chickpeas
Parmesan cheese

In a large soup pot, sauté onion, garlic, parsley, and celery in oil. Cover and cook until tender. Add the remaining ingredients, except beans, chickpeas and noodles.

Cook, covered, for 45 minutes. Add beans, chickpeas and shells. Simmer for 10 minutes. Serve with grated Parmesan cheese on top.

Split Pea Soup

2 cups dried split peas
2 to 3 quarts cold water
1 ham bone
1 onion, diced
3 stalks celery, chopped
3 carrots, chopped thin
1 cup ham, diced
Salt and pepper

Add peas and water to a soup kettle. Add all remaining ingredients except ham. Bring slowly to a boil. Cover and simmer about 4 to 5 hours until peas are tender.

Add ham 1/2 hour before soup is done. Add more water if needed while cooking. Skim off excess fat. Season to taste with salt and pepper.

MISC. SOUPS

Is chicken soup good for your health?

Not if you're the chicken.

Egg Drop Soup

1 tablespoon corn starch
4 cups water
4 teaspoons chicken flavor bouillon
1 egg, well beaten
Sliced green onion to taste

Stir corn starch in 1/2 cup water in a medium saucepan. Combine with chicken bouillon. Cook, stirring occasionally until bouillon dissolves.

Slowly stir in the egg and heat through. Garnish with green onion. Refrigerate leftovers.

Yield: 1 quart.

Mushroom Soup

1/2 cup butter
1/2 cup onion, minced
1 lb. fresh mushrooms, washed, dried, and minced
2 1/2 tablespoons flour
4 1/2 cups beef stock
1 cup light cream
Salt

Garnish:
Paprika
Minced fresh parsley

In a saucepan, over low heat, melt the butter and sauté the onion until soft but not brown, about 15 minutes. Add the mushrooms and sauté for 3 to 4 minutes. Stir in the flour and cook for 1 minute, stirring constantly. Then gradually add the beef stock. Cook and stir until thickened.

Add the cream and heat, but do not boil. Season with salt, then sprinkle with paprika and parsley.

Wonton Soup

1 1/2 lbs. bay or sea scallops, coarsely chopped
1/2 lb. pork, coarsely ground
1/4 lb. ham, coarsely ground
8 canned bamboo shoots, drained and finely minced
6 large Chinese mushrooms, soaked in hot water for 15 to 30 minutes, drained, dried, and finely minced
1 egg
6 tablespoons chopped shallots
2 tablespoons Chinese rice wine or dry sherry
1 teaspoon salt
Freshly ground black pepper to taste
Extra-thin wonton skins
8 cups chicken stock

Combine the first 10 ingredients in a bowl and mix well. Place a wonton skin flour side down on a work surface. Put 1/2 teaspoon of the filling in the center of the wonton skin; don't overstuff. Gently pinch the edges to close and twist the ends to seal. Repeat until all the filling is used.

In a large pot, bring 4 quarts of water to a boil. Add the filled wontons in batches and cook for 2 to 4 minutes. Don't crowd. The wontons will float to the top and look transparent when they are done. Remove the wontons with a slotted spoon and set aside.

Pour the chicken stock in a large saucepan and bring to a simmer. Add the wontons and heat through.

Cold Cucumber Soup

2 8" cucumbers, cut in halves, seeded and cut in pieces
2 tablespoons scallions
2 tablespoons butter
1 tablespoon wine vinegar
1 quart chicken broth
1 tablespoon farina*
Salt
Fresh dill
1/2 cup sour cream
Fresh parsley

Cook the scallions in butter until soft. Add cucumbers and wine vinegar. Add broth, farina and salt to taste, then add a pinch of dill. Simmer for 25 minutes or until cucumbers are soft. Add soup to a blender and puree. Pour the puree into bowl; add sour cream. Beat well with a whisk.

Serve cold.

*Substitutes for farina are cream of wheat, oatmeal, cornmeal, polenta, or couscous.

Onion Soup

3 cups yellow onions (4 large)
6 cups beef broth
1/4 cup butter
2 teaspoons salt
1/4 teaspoon pepper
1/4 cup sugar
2 tablespoons flour

In a large saucepan, over medium-low heat, sauté onions in butter until light brown. Cover and simmer 15 minutes. Add sugar, salt, pepper, broth, flour (mixed with a little broth) and bring to a boil. Simmer 1/2 hour.

Toast French bread, put on top of soup in serving bowls. Sprinkle Swiss or Parmesan cheese on top. Bake 10 minutes in a 425 degrees F. oven.

Wild Rice Soup

2 tablespoons onion, minced
2 tablespoons butter
1/4 cup flour
4 cups chicken broth
1/2 teaspoon salt
2 cups cooked wild rice
1/2 cup ham, minced
1/3 cup carrots, finely grated
2 tablespoons silvered almonds, chopped
1 cup half & half

In a large soup kettle, sauté onion in butter until tender. Mix in flour; gradually add broth. Cook, stirring constantly, until mixture thickens slightly. Stir in salt, rice, ham, carrots and almonds; simmer about 15 minutes or until carrots are tender. Mix in half & half; simmer until hot.

Yield: 6 to 7 cups.

SOUP CROUTONS

Tasty Garlic Croutons

1/4 cup butter
1 minced clove of garlic
3 slices of French bread, about 1" thick

In a large non-stick skillet, on medium heat, melt butter. Mix in minced garlic and stir for 1 minute. Place cubed breadcrumbs in butter and toss to evenly coat.

Spread out bread cubes on a baking sheet, bake in preheated 350 degrees F. oven for 15 minutes. Check often to prevent the croutons from burning.

Easy Crouton Recipe

5 slices of bread (wheat or white), cubed
4 tablespoons of olive oil

Preheat oven to 350 degrees F. Place cubed bread in a large mixing bowl. Drizzle olive oil over bread cubes and toss until lightly coated.

Layer bread cubes on a baking sheet and bake at 350 degrees F. until golden & crispy, approximately 15 to 20 minutes. Turn once about halfway through. Let croutons cool before serving.

CHILI

Turkey Chili

1 lb. ground turkey
3 tablespoons onion
1 teaspoon salt
1 (15 oz.) can ranch style beans, drained and washed
3 teaspoons chili powder
1 (10.75 oz.) can condensed tomato soup

Cook turkey, onion and salt in a 2-quart saucepan, stirring occasionally until turkey is no longer pink; drain.

Add beans, chili powder, tomato soup and one soup can of water. Heat to boiling, stirring occasionally.

PIZZA CHILI

1 lb. ground beef
1 (16 oz.) can red beans, drained
1 (15 oz.) can pizza sauce
1 (46 oz.) can spicy vegetable juice
1/2 pkg. pepperoni, diced or sausage, browned
1 teaspoon pizza seasoning or Italian seasoning
1 teaspoon salt
Shredded mozzarella cheese

In a large saucepan, brown ground beef. Add remaining ingredients except cheese; simmer for 30 minutes. Garnish servings with mozzarella cheese.

Yield: 8 servings.

Chicken Chili

4 onions, chopped
2 green peppers, chopped
3 cloves garlic, diced
2 teaspoons cooking oil
1 chicken, cooked and diced
1 teaspoon cumin
1 teaspoon oregano
1/2 teaspoon coriander
1/2 teaspoon thyme
1/2 lb. hamburger, browned
2 bay leaves
3 teaspoons chili powder
1 (6 oz.) can tomato paste
3 (28 oz.) cans tomatoes
1 teaspoon salt
1 teaspoon pepper

In large stock pot, sauté onions, green peppers and garlic in oil until onions are transparent. Add cooked chicken and sauté a few more minutes. Add cumin, oregano, coriander, thyme, browned hamburger, bay leaves, chili powder, tomato paste, tomatoes, salt, and pepper; simmer for at least an hour for the best flavor. Add water if chili seems too thick.

Serve with shredded cheese, sour cream, green onions, and tortilla chips, if desired.

Basic Ranch Chili

1 lb. ground beef
2 cloves garlic, minced
1 onion, chopped
1 teaspoon salt
1 teaspoon oregano
1 tablespoon chili powder
1 (8 oz.) can tomato sauce
2 (14.5 oz. each) cans stewed tomatoes
1/2 (15 oz.) can kidney beans

In a large stock pot, cook ground beef, garlic and onion until beef is browned; drain.

Mix in salt, oregano, chili powder, tomato sauce and tomatoes. Heat to boiling, cover, reduce heat and simmer.

Cook for one hour, stirring frequently. Stir in beans. Simmer for an additional 15 minutes.

SANDWICHES

TUNA SANDWICHES

Stacked Tuna & Bacon Sandwich

2 (5 oz. each) cans albacore tuna
1 teaspoon Dijon mustard
2 tablespoons pickle relish
1 teaspoon horseradish
2 tablespoons red onion, chopped
1/2 teaspoon paprika
Salt and pepper to taste
4 hoagie buns, split
2 ripe avocados, peeled and sliced
2 tomatoes, sliced
4 slices of provolone cheese
4 lettuce leaves
8 bacon slices, cooked and crumbled

In a medium bowl, combine tuna, mustard, relish, horseradish and red onion. Sprinkle with paprika, salt and pepper.

Evenly divide mixture between 4 hoagie buns. Top with equal amounts of avocado, tomatoes, a slice of cheese, lettuce leaf and bacon.

Tuna or Crab Sandwiches

1 (5 oz.) can tuna or crab
1/4 cup mayonnaise
3 oz. cream cheese
1 egg yolk
1 teaspoon onion, chopped
1/4 teaspoon mustard
3 English muffins split and buttered

In a small bowl, stir fish and mayonnaise together. Spread on muffins.

Beat together cream cheese, egg yolk, onion, mustard. Spoon mixture over fish and spread. Broil 3 minutes or until browned.

Hot Tuna and Cheese Sandwich

1 (5 oz.) can tuna
1/4 cup butter or margarine
1 teaspoon prepared mustard
6 slices bread
1 teaspoon onion, minced
1/2 cup celery, chopped
1 teaspoon sweet pickle relish
1/4 cup mayonnaise
6 slices sharp American cheese
Paprika, if desired

Drain tuna. Flake in a bowl. In another bowl, cream butter and blend in mustard. Spread bread slices with mustard butter. Add remaining ingredients, except cheese and paprika to the flaked tuna, tossing with enough mayonnaise to moisten the mixture.

Spread buttered bread with tuna mixture and cover with cheese. Sprinkle lightly with paprika, if desired, and place on baking sheet. Bake in a very hot oven, 450 degrees, for 10 to 12 minutes, or until cheese melts and bread toasts lightly.

Yield: 6 servings.

Tasty Tuna Sandwich

1 (5 oz.) can tuna drained
1 cup cottage cheese, drained
1/2 cup shredded Cheddar cheese
1/3 cup mayonnaise
1 cup shredded carrots or alfalfa sprouts
2 hard cooked eggs, chopped
1/4 cup celery, chopped
1 medium tomato, chopped
1 teaspoon lemon-pepper
8 lettuce leaves

In a large bowl, combine tuna, cottage cheese, cheddar cheese, tomato, eggs and celery. Stir mayonnaise and lemon-pepper together. Add to tuna mixture; stir until mixed.

If using carrots, add them to the tuna mixture, but if using sprouts, put them on top of the filling in the sandwich. Top with a lettuce leaf.

Yield: 8 sandwiches (1/3 to 1/2 cup of filling each)

Hot Tuna Sandwiches

1 (5 oz.) can tuna
1/4 lb. cheese, cubed
2 teaspoons finely onion, chopped
2 teaspoons green pepper
3 hardboiled eggs, cut up
2 teaspoons sweet pickles, cut up
2 teaspoons stuffed olives, cut up
1/4 cup mayonnaise

In a medium bowl, combine all ingredients. Spread on 12 to 14 hamburger buns or coney buns. Wrap in foil and bake 30 minutes at 250 degrees.

HAM SANDWICHES

Hot Ham and Swiss

8 slices Swiss cheese
24 thin slices ham
2 tablespoons soft butter
1 teaspoon poppy seeds
1 teaspoon Dijon mustard
2 tablespoons minced onion
4 onion rolls or other bakery buns

In a small bowl, combine butter, poppy seeds, mustard and onion; spread on split buns. Layer ham and cheese on buns.

Wrap in foil and bake 15 minutes in a 350 degrees F. oven until cheese melts. Can make ahead and freeze.

Yield: 4 sandwiches.

Baked Ham Sliders

1/2 cup melted butter or margarine
1 tablespoon spicy brown mustard
1 teaspoon Worcestershire sauce
2 tablespoons grated onion
2 teaspoons poppy seeds
12 slider buns
1/2 lb. thinly sliced deli ham
1/2 lb. thinly sliced Swiss cheese

In a medium bowl, combine butter, mustard, Worcestershire sauce, onion, and poppy seeds.

Spray a 9x13-inch baking dish with non-stick cooking spray. Separate the bottoms from the tops of the slider buns. Arrange slider bottoms in the baking dish. Layer half the ham slices on the slider bottoms. Add a layer of Swiss cheese, top with remaining ham slices. Add the tops of sliders on top of ham layer.

Pour the butter mixture evenly over the sliders. Spread the mixture a little on top with a basting brush or knife.

Bake in preheated 350 degrees F. oven for about 20 minutes, until cheese has melted, and sliders have lightly browned. Use a knife to slice through the layers to create 12 individual servings.

Serve with chips and a pickle.

Baked Ham Sandwiches

1/2 cup ham, chopped
1 cup Velveeta cheese, cubed
4 hardboiled eggs
1 cup celery, diced
1/2 cup onions, diced
4 tablespoons salad dressing
2 tablespoons vinegar

In a large bowl, combine all ingredients. Spread mixture on buns, wrap in foil. Bake at 375 degrees F. for 10 minutes.

Ham & Cheese Roll Ups

1 can crescent dinner rolls
8 slices cooked ham, thinly sliced
4 slices cheddar cheese, thinly sliced

Preheat oven to 350 degrees F. Cut each slice of cheese into 4 strips. Lay crescent rolls out in 8 triangles. Add a single slice of ham to each triangle. Take 2 strips of cheese and lay them on the center of the ham slice. Tuck in the edges of the ham to line up with the crescent roll. Roll up crescents from wide end down to the tip and put on baking sheet, tip down.

Bake 15 to 20 minutes at 350 degrees F. or until crescents are golden brown.

CHEESE SANDWICHES

Extreme Grilled Cheese

1 (3 oz.) package cream cheese, softened
3/4 cup mayonnaise
1 (4 oz.) package cheddar cheese, shredded
1 (4 oz.) package mozzarella cheese, shredded
1/8 teaspoon seasoned salt
1/2 teaspoon garlic powder
10 slices Italian bread, 1/2" thick
2 teaspoons margarine, softened

In a mixing bowl, beat mayonnaise and cream cheese until smooth. Stir in cheese, salt and garlic powder.

Spread 1/3 cup of cheese mixture on 5 slices of bread. Add the other bread slice on top. Spread the margarine on the outsides of the bread; cook in a large skillet over medium heat until golden brown on both sides.

Yield: 5 servings.

Grilled Tomato & Cheese Sandwiches

4 teaspoons butter, softened
4 slices bread
4 (1 oz. each) slices Colby Jack cheese
4 slices tomato (1/4 to 1/2 inch thick)

Spread butter on one side of each of the four slices of bread. On two bread slices, butter side facing down, layer one slice of cheese, two tomato slices and another slice of cheese. Add the other bread slice on top with the buttered side facing up.

Heat a 12-inch skillet over medium heat. Add sandwiches; cook about 3 minutes or until the bottom lightly browns. Turn and cook about 3 minutes longer or until golden brown and cheese is melted.

Peanut Butter and Cheese Sandwiches

4 slices white bread
4 slices of bacon, cooked and drained
2 tablespoons peanut butter
2 tablespoons margarine
2 slices Velvetta or American cheese

Spread 1 tablespoon peanut butter on each of 2 slices of bread. Add the cheese slice and 2 slices of bacon. Add the other bread slice on top. Spread the margarine on the outsides of the bread; cook in a large skillet over medium heat until golden brown on both sides.

CHICKEN & TURKEY SANDWICHES

Chipotle Chicken Sandwich

If Chipotle peppers are too hot for you, this sandwich is also great with just mayo.

4 cooked chicken breasts, sliced if too thick
1 tablespoon canned chipotle peppers, finely chopped
2 tablespoons mayonnaise
4 pieces American cheese
4 lettuce leaves
8 slices rye or wheat bread, toasted
1 tomato, sliced

In a small bowl, combine peppers and mayo. Have the tomato and lettuce sliced and ready to go. Heat precooked chicken breast (or use cooked frozen chicken breasts – heated per instructions on package.)

Toast the bread. Add a lettuce leaf, tomato slices, 1 piece of cheese and a chicken breast to 4 slices of toast. Spread the peppered mayo on the other 4 slices of toast and place on top of the chicken breast.

Yield: 4 sandwiches.

Triple-Decker Sandwich

1/2 lb. cooked turkey breast slices, thinly sliced
8 large iceberg lettuce leaves
2 tomatoes, sliced
12 slices white or wheat bread
16 slices bacon
1/3 cup mayonnaise
1/4 teaspoon salt
1/8 teaspoon pepper

Cook the bacon and toast the bread slices. Set aside.

In a small bowl, stir together the mayonnaise, salt and pepper. Spread the mixture on the toast slices.

Assembly – On four of the bread slices, place an equal amount of the turkey and then half of the lettuce. Next add the 2nd piece of bread on top of the sandwich with mayonnaise side up. Add the tomato slices and then 4 bacon slices on each sandwich. Then add the remaining lettuce and the other 4 bread slices (putting the side with the mayonnaise down) on top. Press down gently on the sandwiches and hold them together with toothpicks. Slice into quarters or halves.

Yield: 4 sandwiches.

Luncheon Sandwiches

Layer:

Toasted bread slices
Mayonnaise
Chicken chunks
Jellied cranberry sauce, drop by teaspoon
Shredded Swiss cheese

Broil until cheese melts.

Variation: Toast and mayonnaise, slice of ham, pineapple slice and shredded Swiss cheese.

MISCELLANEOUS SANDWICHES

Big Sandwich

1 rounded loaf sourdough bread, unsliced
2 teaspoons ketchup
1/2 lb. deli roast beef, sliced thin
2 teaspoons yellow mustard
1/2 lb. deli ham or turkey, sliced thin
4 slices Swiss cheese or 3 t. crumbled feta cheese
2 teaspoons mayonnaise
1 small tomato, sliced thin
4 bacon strips, cooked
4 slices American cheese
2 or 3 teaspoons chopped red onion
2 teaspoons butter, melted
1/2 teaspoon onion salt

Slice bread horizontally in 5 equal layers. Assemble on baking sheet in the following layers:

Layer 1: Spread ketchup on bottom layer of bread and top with thinly sliced roast beef. Next add a layer of bread.

Layer 2: Spread mustard and top with the ham or turkey slices and Swiss or Feta cheese. Cover with next layer of bread.

Layer 3: Spread mayonnaise and top with tomato slices and bacon strips. Cover with next layer of bread.

Layer 4: Add American cheese and chopped red onion. Cover with top layer of bread. **Layer 5:** Brush melted butter on top and sides of loaf; sprinkle with onion salt. Loosely tent with aluminum foil. Bake at 350 degrees for 30 minutes, or until heated through. Remove from oven and let stand 10 minutes. Carefully slice into wedges with an electric knife.

STROMBOLI

1 loaf frozen bread dough, thawed
1 cup cheddar cheese, shredded
1 cup mozzarella cheese, shredded
1 (5 oz.) package pepperoni slices
1 cup ham, chopped or sliced
1 (6 oz.) package Canadian bacon slices

Roll out thawed bread dough loaf on a large, baking sheet sprayed with cooking spray. Add all ingredients down the center of entire loaf. Fold and pinch all sides and ends. Bake at 350 degrees F. for 15 to 25 minutes.

Optional: Spread a light coating of melted butter on the top just before serving.

Serve with chips and a pickle. Can be dipped in pizza sauce.

Low Calorie Salad Sandwich

2 slices whole wheat toast
1/2 teaspoon mayonnaise
6 slices cucumber
1/4 firm tomato, sliced
1/4 onion, sliced
1/4 green pepper, sliced
3 mushrooms, thinly sliced
1/8 large apple, sliced
1 Kosher dill pickle

Spread mayonnaise on both pieces of toast. Layer the rest of the ingredients (except pickle) on toast and serve with pickle.

Swedish Open-Faced Sandwiches

Small loaf of rye or pumpernickel bread
Whipped butter

Butter the bread lightly. The point of this open-faced sandwich is to please the eye as well as the palate with contrasting colors and shapes. Below are some of the toppings you can use to make a great looking open-faced sandwich.

Meat – thin slices of roast beef, ham, chicken or turkey or chopped meat made into ham, chicken or turkey salad.

Hard-cooked eggs – sliced and placed on the bread in overlapping rows or made into egg salad.

Seafood – shrimp or tuna salad.

Cheese – again, thin slices, overlapping; cheddar, Colby, Swiss, or brown-edged smoked cheese. Also could use cream cheese with sliced olives on top.

To assemble – top each piece of bread with desired toppings and cut in half. Do not place bread on top of filling but leave it as an open-faced sandwich.

Sloppy Joes for 24

3 1/2 lbs. ground beef
2/3 cup of milk
1 1/4 cups of onion, chopped
1/2 tablespoon pepper
1 1/4 tablespoon salt

Brown ingredients above in a large skillet or large pot – Add:

1 (20 oz.) bottle ketchup
1 cup water
1 1/4 tablespoon Worchester sauce
1 1/4 tablespoon vinegar
1 1/4 tablespoon sugar
1/2 cup or more tomato juice

Simmer 1 hour or more until spreading consistency. Serve on toasted buns.

Yield: 24 servings.

Olympic Gold Sandwich

10 hardboiled eggs
1/2 cup carrots shredded
1/2 cup French dressing
1/2 cup celery, chopped
3 green onions, chopped
1/4 teaspoon salt
6 Kaiser rolls
Mayonnaise
6 lettuce leaves
6 slices of tomato
12 cucumber slices

In a medium bowl, chop eggs; add carrots, French dressing, celery, onions, and salt. Stir to blend.

Cut Kaiser rolls in half lengthwise, hollow out centers. Spread each half with a small amount of mayonnaise; spread 1/2 cup of egg mixture on each half roll. Top the bottom halves with lettuce, tomato, and cucumber slices. Replace top and serve.

Ribeye Sandwiches

1 ribeye or eye of round steak, 5 to 6 lbs.
Small French rolls
1/2 teaspoon crushed cardamom
1/4 cup coarse black pepper
1/2 teaspoon garlic powder
1 teaspoon paprika
1 tablespoon tomato paste
3/4 cup vinegar
1 cup soy sauce

In a small bowl, combine cardamom and pepper; press the mixture on the meat. Place meat in a dish. In another bowl, combine garlic powder, paprika and tomato paste. Add vinegar and soy sauce, blend well.

Pour marinade over meat and marinate in the refrigerator overnight, turning occasionally.

Preheat oven to 300 degrees F. Remove the meat from the marinade and drain. Wrap the meat in foil and roast in a pan for 2 hours. Serve thinly sliced in small French rolls.

Yield: Serves 10 to 12.

Round Sandwich

Large loaf of round French bread
2 large tomatoes, sliced
1/2 lb. assorted sliced luncheon meat
3 oz. sliced turkey pepperoni
1/4 lb. assorted cheeses, sliced
1 (2.25 oz.) can sliced ripe black olives, drained
3 large dill pickles, sliced lengthwise
1 onion, sliced
Mayonnaise

Cut bread horizontally in 2 pieces. Hollow out the soft bread from each half, leaving an exterior shell of about 1/2 to 3/4 inches thick. Spread mayonnaise on the bread shells.

On the bottom bread crust, layer meat, pepperoni, cheese, half of the tomatoes, olives, pickles and onion. Top with the rest of the tomatoes and place the top crust on the filling; press together firmly. Cut in wedges to serve.

Yield: 8 servings.

SEAFOOD

Lobster Crab Sandwiches

1 (3 oz.) can lobster meat
1 (6 oz.) can crabmeat
8 oz. finely shredded sharp cheddar cheese
Onion to taste
Celery to taste
3 slices bacon, crisp and crumbled
Mayonnaise

In a medium bowl, mix all ingredients until moist. Spread on 1/2 hamburger buns. Bake in oven for 30 minutes at 350 degrees F.

Crab Delight Sandwich

8 oz. crab, flaked
1 1/2 teaspoons prepared mustard
1/2 teaspoon Worcestershire sauce
1 1/2 teaspoons onion, grated
2 teaspoons green pepper, chopped
1/2 cup mayonnaise, scant
6 slices white bread
8 small tomatoes, discard the ends and cut in 24 slices
1/2 cup mayonnaise
1/4 cup finely shredded cheese

Lightly toast bread and remove crusts. Cut into 24 squares.

In a medium bowl, combine crab, mustard, Worcestershire sauce, onion, green pepper and mayonnaise. Pile on the lightly toasted bread.

Top each bread section with 1 tomato slice. Add 2nd mayonnaise and cheese on top of tomato. Broil 4" from heat until topping puffs and browns slightly.

Yield: 24 appetizers.

Party Shrimp Burgers

3 (6.5 oz.) cans broken shrimp
2 1/2 cups celery, chopped
2 bunches green onions
8 oz. Cheddar cheese
4 hard-boiled eggs, separated and mashed
1 cup mayonnaise
Buns

In a medium bowl, mix all ingredients together and spread on bun halves. Top with cheese; put in oven or under broiler until cheese melts and sandwich is warm.

Yield: Mixture for 30 buns.

WRAPS

CHICKEN AND TURKEY WRAPS

Caesar Salad & Chicken Wrap

4 flour tortillas
3 cups romaine lettuce, shredded
4 slices cooked bacon, crumbled
2 cups cooked chicken, chopped
1/4 cup Parmesan cheese, shredded
1/4 cup croutons
1/2 cup Caesar dressing

In a large mixing bowl, stir together the lettuce, bacon, chicken, cheese and croutons. Add the Caesar dressing and toss. Spoon even portions onto each tortilla and roll tightly. Cut rolled tortillas in half.

Turkey & Bacon Wrap

Turkey & Bacon Wrap

2 tablespoons of Dijon or plain mustard
1 (8 oz.) package cream cheese with chives
6 tortillas, whole wheat
1 1/2 cups of lettuce, finely shredded iceberg
12 slices of deli turkey, sliced thin
3/4 cup Swiss cheese, shredded
1 diced large tomato
1 sliced large avocado
6 slices of cooked bacon, crumbled
1 bunch of green onions, chopped

In a small bowl, combine mustard and cream cheese. On each whole wheat tortilla spread approximately 2 tablespoons of the mustard and cream cheese mixture.

Sprinkle 1/4 cup of the shredded lettuce on the tortilla and press lettuce into the cream cheese and mustard mixture. Add 2 of the turkey slices on top of the lettuce. Add green onions and shredded Swiss cheese on top. On each tortilla, add a portion of the crumbled bacon, sliced avocado and diced tomato. Tightly roll all 6 tortillas. Cut in half using a diagonal cut.

Holiday Turkey Wrap

1/2 cup chive and onion cream cheese
1/2 cup dried cranberries
1 small bag of spinach
1/2 lb. of turkey, shredded
4 spinach or herb wraps
8 slices of Swiss cheese

Spread cream cheese on each spinach wrap. Put a generous portion of turkey on top of cream cheese and add a layer of spinach leaves. Add 2 slices of Swiss cheese on top of spinach and sprinkle with dried cranberries. Roll each wrap, cut in half and serve.

Turkey and Veggie Wrap

4 flour tortillas
8 slices turkey breast
1/2 cup cucumber, thinly sliced
1/2 red bell pepper, sliced strips
4 tablespoons mayonnaise
1/4 teaspoon oregano
1/4 teaspoon garlic powder

In a small bowl, stir together mayonnaise, oregano and garlic powder and spread an even layer over each tortilla. Add 2 slices of turkey on top of mayonnaise. Add cucumber and red bell pepper on top of turkey. Roll filled tortillas and serve.

Lunch Time Turkey Wrap

4 tablespoons honey mustard
12 oz. deli turkey, thinly sliced
4 slices of Muenster cheese
1 cup fresh baby spinach
2 carrots, shredded
2 strips of cooked bacon, crumbled
1/2 cup cucumber, chopped
1/2 cup roasted sweet red pepper, chopped
4 whole wheat tortillas, 8 inches

Spread a layer of honey mustard on each tortilla. Next layer a portion of turkey, Muenster cheese, bacon, carrot, cucumber and roasted pepper. Roll each tortilla tightly and cut in half diagonally.

Chicken With Peanut Butter Wrap

1/4 cup creamy peanut butter
1/4 cup grape jelly
1/4 cup plain yogurt
4 tortillas, whole wheat
12 oz. shredded chicken
8 slices bacon, crumbled
4 leaves of romaine lettuce
2 peeled carrots, grated
2 small red bell peppers, sliced

Mix peanut butter and jelly together in a microwave safe bowl and microwave for 1 minute. Stir in plain yogurt.

On each tortilla spread a layer of the peanut butter mixture. Add even portions of the remaining ingredients. Roll filled tortilla, lay folded side down on plate and cut in half.

Tuscan Chicken Wrap

1 (16 oz.) package stir-fry frozen vegetable blend
2 (6 oz. each) packages grilled chicken breast strips
1/2 cup Italian salad dressing
1/4 cup Parmesan cheese, shredded
6 flour tortillas, room temperature

In a saucepan, cook frozen stir fry veggies according to the directions on the package and drain. Add cooked chicken breast, cheese and Italian dressing to the pan. Simmer for 3 to 4 minutes uncovered.

Put 3/4 cup of heated chicken mixture on each tortilla. Roll the filled tortillas and serve.

Southwest Chicken Wrap

6 10-inch tortillas
3 to 4 tablespoons pickled jalapenos, chopped
1 cup sour cream
3 tablespoons fresh lime juice
Salt and pepper to taste
4 cups of cooked chicken, shredded
1 small bag of baby spinach
1 (15 oz.) can of black beans, drained and rinsed
1 large tomato, sliced thin
1 red onion, sliced thin
1 avocado, sliced thin

In a small bowl, mix jalapenos, sour cream and lime juice; add salt and pepper. Spread sour cream mixture on tortillas.

On each wrap, layer equal portions of chicken, spinach, beans, tomato, onion and avocado. Roll tightly and place seam side down on plate.

Turkey Chipotle Wrap

1/2 cup mayonnaise
1 tablespoon chipotle chilies in adobo sauce, chopped
2 teaspoons adobo sauce
4 10-inch wheat tortillas
1/2 lb. smoked turkey, sliced
1 cup Monterey jack cheese, shredded
1 peeled avocado, sliced
4 leaves of romaine lettuce

In a small bowl, mix together the adobo sauce, chipotle chilies and mayonnaise. Evenly spread mayonnaise mixture on each tortilla. In even proportions, place lettuce leaf, turkey, cheese and avocado on all 4 tortillas. Tightly roll each filled tortilla and cut in half.

South of the Border Chicken Wrap

8 flour tortillas
1 lb. chicken breast, boneless
2 cups water
1 cup chunky salsa
1 (2 oz.) package taco seasoning
1 tablespoon oil
1 (8 oz.) package Santa Fe or Spanish ready rice
2 cups cheddar cheese, shredded

In a deep skillet, fry chicken in oil until lightly browned. Cut chicken into strips and return to skillet. Pour 2 cups of water, taco seasoning and salsa over chicken and heat until boiling. Mix in rice, cover skillet and reduce heat. Cook on low heat for 5 minutes.

Put spoonfuls of mixture on each tortilla, sprinkle with cheese and roll tightly.

Delicious Chicken Wrap

3 cups cooked chicken breast, shredded
1 cup coleslaw in a bag (without any sauce)
3/4 teaspoon chili powder
1 teaspoon lime juice
1/2 cup Ranch dressing
1/2 cup Pepper Jack cheese, shredded
1/2 cup cherry tomatoes, cut in half
8 or 10 flour tortillas, warmed
Salsa
Sour cream

In a large bowl, mix together chicken, lime juice, dressing, chili powder, tomatoes, coleslaw and cheese.

Spoon on warmed tortillas and top with sour cream and salsa. Roll tortillas and serve.

VEGGIE WRAPS

Easy Veggie Wrap

1/2 cup spreadable cream cheese, garlic/herb
4 tortillas, whole wheat or flour
1 cup fresh baby spinach
1 cup tomatoes, chopped
3/4 cup green or red bell pepper, chopped
4 strips of cooked bacon, crumbled
Salt and pepper to taste

Spread a layer of the spreadable cheese evenly over all 4 tortillas. Top with spinach, tomatoes, bell pepper, bacon and salt and pepper. Roll tortillas tightly and serve.

Avocado Wrap

2 ripe avocados, peeled & sliced thin
4 wheat tortillas
2 cups shredded lettuce
2 medium tomatoes, sliced thin
1/2 cup Parmesan cheese, shredded
1/2 teaspoon garlic powder
Salt and pepper to taste

Using a fork, mash one of the avocados in a small bowl and spread 1/4 of the mashed avocado on each tortilla. Continue layering ingredients on tortilla as follows: lettuce, avocado slices and tomato slices.

Sprinkle garlic powder, salt and pepper and cheese on top and roll tortilla tightly.

Black Bean & Veggie Wrap

4 tortillas, flour
1 (15 oz.) can black beans, drained and rinsed
1 bag of fresh baby spinach
1/2 cup Monterey Jack cheese, shredded
2 cups of fresh mushrooms, sliced
1 small purple onion, diced
Cooking spray

Spray a non-stick skillet with cooking spray and heat skillet over medium/high heat. Add mushrooms and chopped onions to the heated skillet. Stir frequently until the onions are tender. Add the beans to the skillet and cook until heated. Remove from heat.

Warm tortillas in microwave and put a portion of bean mixture on each tortilla, top with spinach and cheese. Roll tortillas and serve.

Simple Salad Wrap

4 flour tortillas
1/2 cup cheddar cheese, shredded
2 cups of your favorite veggies, chopped
4 tablespoons of ranch dressing
1/4 cup almonds, sliced
Salt & pepper

On flour tortillas, put an equal portion of veggies, almonds and cheese. Top veggies with ranch dressing, salt and pepper to taste and roll up.

TUNA WRAPS

Spicy Tuna Wrap

2 (5 oz. each) cans of tuna in water, drained
1/3 cup mayonnaise or salad dressing
1 tablespoon of hot sauce
1/4 cup onion
2 cups brown rice, cooked
2 tablespoons rice or wine vinegar
4 10-inch wheat wraps
3 cups spinach leaves, chopped
1 avocado, cut into slices

In a medium bowl, stir together tuna, mayonnaise, onions & hot sauce. In a small bowl, combine rice and vinegar. Spread the tuna mixture over all 4 wraps. Place desired amounts of rice, spinach leaves and avocado slices on each tortilla. Roll wraps tightly and dip in soy sauce.

Tasty Tuna Wrap

1 (5 oz.) can of tuna in water, drained
1/4 cup mayonnaise
2 teaspoons lemon juice
2 tablespoons basil pesto
Salt and pepper
1/2 cup shredded lettuce
2 slices provolone cheese, cut in half
10 salad or black olives, cut in half
2 10-inch flour tortillas

In a medium bowl, mix together tuna, mayonnaise, lemon juice and basil pesto. Add salt and pepper to taste. Spread the mixture over the tortillas. Add lettuce, cheese & olives on top of the tuna. Roll wraps tightly.

Tuna Crunch Wrap

1/4 cup mayonnaise
4 1/4 teaspoons prepared mustard
4 spinach or wheat tortillas
2 (7 oz. each) pouches of tuna in water
1/2 cup green onions, chopped
1/2 cup water chestnuts, chopped
3/4 cup red pepper, chopped
1/2 cup celery, finely chopped
2 cups lettuce, shredded
1/2 cup cheddar cheese, shredded

Combine mustard & mayonnaise in a small bowl. Stir in the tuna, onions, water chestnuts, red pepper and celery. Spread mixture over each tortilla, top with shredded lettuce and cheese and roll wraps tightly.

Southwest Tuna Wrap

2 12-inch wheat tortillas
1 pouch or (5 oz.) can of tuna, packed in water
1 (15 oz.) can black beans, drained
1/2 cup salsa, hot or mild
3/4 cup iceberg lettuce, shredded
1/2 cup cheddar cheese, shredded

On each tortilla layer ingredients as follows: tuna, black beans, salsa, lettuce and cheddar cheese. Roll wraps tightly.

SPICED TUNA WRAP

1 (5 oz.) can of tuna in water, drained
6 tablespoons mayonnaise
1/8 teaspoon garlic powder
1 tablespoon dried parsley
1 teaspoon dill weed
1/2 (2.25 oz.) can sliced ripe olives
1/3 cup cheddar cheese, shredded
1/2 cup shredded lettuce
2 10 or 12-inch wheat tortillas

In a medium bowl, combine tuna, mayonnaise, garlic powder, parsley and dill weed. Add olives and cheese and mix. Spread the mixture over the tortillas. Add lettuce on top of the tuna. Roll wraps tightly.

Yield: 1 1/2 12" wraps or 2 smaller wraps.

DESSERT WRAPS

Chocolate & Peanut Butter Wrap

4 8-inch flour tortillas
1/2 cup creamy peanut butter
1/2 cup mini semisweet chocolate chips
1 cup mini marshmallows
Ice cream, vanilla or chocolate
Chocolate syrup

Spread equal amounts of peanut butter on all 4 tortillas. On half of each tortilla, sprinkle mini marshmallows and mini chocolate chips. Roll tortilla up tightly beginning with the side that only has peanut butter. Heat tortillas in microwave for 30 seconds to 1 minute or until heated through. Serve with ice cream and drizzle with chocolate syrup.

Apple Cinnamon Wrap

3 apples, peeled and chopped
3 tablespoons butter
1 1/2 teaspoons cinnamon
3 tablespoons sugar
4 10-inch flour tortillas
Powdered sugar
Vanilla ice cream

Melt butter in a small skillet. Add the chopped apples to the skillet along with the cinnamon and sugar. Stir and cook until apples are tender but not mushy. Remove skillet from heat. Place 3/4 cup of mixture on one side of each tortilla. Slightly fold over bottom and top of each tortilla then roll it up. Cut each wrap at an angle, dust with powdered sugar and serve with a scoop of vanilla ice cream.

Grilled Sweet Tortillas

1/2 cup almond butter
4 8-inch flour tortillas
1 cup mini marshmallows
1/2 cup flaked coconut
1/2 cup of chocolate chips
Whipped topping

Spread almond butter on tortillas. On half of each tortilla, layer even portions of marshmallows, coconut and chocolate chips. Roll tortilla starting with filled side. Wrap tortillas in foil and grill over low heat for 5 to 10 minutes or microwave until heated through. Serve topped with whipped topping.

Hey, if you loved this book and want to get more recipes like this, subscribe to the newsletter for free at:

http://www.BonnieScottAuthor.com/subscribe.html

Other Books by Bonnie Scott

IN JARS SERIES – InJars.com

100 Easy Recipes in Jars
100 More Easy Recipes in Jars
Desserts in Jars
Easy Desserts and Recipes in Jars – 3 Cookbook Set

CAMPING – CampingFreebies.com

100 Easy Camping Recipes
Camping Recipes: Foil Packet Cooking
Camping Recipes – 2 Cookbook Set

WINTER – NorthPoleChristmas.com

120 Hot Chocolate Recipes
Holiday Recipes: 150 Easy Gifts From Your Kitchen

All titles available in Paperback and Kindle versions at Amazon.com

More Books by Bonnie Scott

Bacon Cookbook: 150 Easy Bacon Recipes

Slow Cooker Comfort Foods

150 Easy Classic Chicken Recipes

Grill It! 125 Easy Recipes

Simply Fleece

Fish & Game Cookbook

Cookie Indulgence: 150 Easy Cookie Recipes

Pies and Mini Pies

A Taste of Italy: Authentic Italian Recipes

The Best Pasta Cookbook: 100 Classic Pasta Recipes

Chocolate Bliss: 150 Easy Chocolate Recipes

Cozy Fall Baking Recipes

Winning Chili Recipes

Pumpkin Obsession: 100 Addictive Fall Pumpkin Recipes

4 Ingredient Cookbook: 150 Quick & Easy Recipes

5 Ingredient Cookbook: Timesaving Recipes

Ice Pop Stars! Popsicle Recipes

The Healthy Cookbook: Simple Homestyle Recipes